The
Courage
to
Care

The Courage to Care

Marilyn Brown Oden

Abingdon
Nashville

THE COURAGE TO CARE

Book Designer: L. B. Wooten

Library of Congress Cataloging in Publication Data
ODEN, MARILYN BROWN.
The courage to care.
    1. Christian life—Methodist authors. 2. Courage. I.
Title.
    BV4501.2.0324   248'.48'7   78-13008

ISBN 0-687-09760-6

MANUFACTURED BY THE PARTHENON PRESS AT
NASHVILLE, TENNESSEE, UNITED STATES OF AMERICA

To Donna Pendarvis

Preface

I would like to express appreciation to the Oklahoma Conference United Methodist Women, whose invitation to lead their annual retreat prompted the initial preparation of part of this material—and whose response to it encouraged me to write this book.

I am indebted to four persons who helped determine the direction of this writing:

—Douglas McPherson, old friend and current church school teacher *cum laude,* whose division of the *Confessions of St. Augustine* into self-awareness, self-understanding, life under God, and the life with God, I adapted in my structure.

—June Warren (Mrs. Chester), who introduced me to Thomas Kelly's *Testament of Devotion.*

—Thomas C. Oden, mentor and member of our extended family, whose book *Game Free* was influential in the last chapter.

—Marilyn Ogilvie, whose review of the rough draft was highly valuable to me in preparing the final copy.

I would like to acknowledge several people who express a courage to care through their commitment to public education:

—The faculty of Whittier Middle School, Norman, Oklahoma—especially Frank Addison, innovative principal, and Bev Brewer, model teacher—with whom I shared my life journey for three years.

—The professional educators who are sharing my journey now and who stand out in their concern for students in the Oklahoma City Public Schools.

—The parent and community volunteers who are helping to build a home/school/community partnership that is vital to urban public education.

—Two persons who share my struggle to strengthen that partnership, Shirley Shanker and Flo Pricer, who serve with me on the School Volunteer Services staff.

I also want to express appreciation to my family—both church and immediate—whose care undergirds my life:

—The members of Crown Heights United Methodist Church, a family diverse in age and ideology and style of expressing their faith, but who stand together in a steadfast love for the church.

—My children, Danna Lee, Dirk, Valerie, and Bryant, who help me to grow as they grow.

—Bill, with whom I am blessed to share a "creative covenant."

All of these people touch my life in meaningful ways, and I am deeply grateful.

Marilyn Brown Oden
Oklahoma City, Oklahoma

Contents

I

Courage
in a Cache-Time

It was over two months ago. The plane soared through the blue winter sky, on course. Pilot was flying Father, Mother, Son, and Friend back through the mountains after a day of skiing. Affluence had taught them to expect comfort and to take power and prestige for granted. From their vantage point high in the sky, they looked down on the rugged Rocky Mountains. All was well.

It was over two decades ago. The planet swirled through the atmosphere, on course. It was a time of "Happy Days" and national supremacy. Our frontier spirit and abundant natural resources had resulted in power, prestige, pride. National comfort blinded us to a world of discomfort. All was well.

Unknown to the flyers, it was time to prepare. But they used that time to reminisce. To reminisce about bolting down the mountains. To relive the day: twisting down the slopes on long slender skis, floating over moguls, gliding around deep-rooted trees, demonstrating their skill on the most difficult runs, and then sitting in the warming house by the big stone fireplace. As they reminisced, they ate and drank and celebrated.

Farewell, Aspen!

It was time for us to prepare. To prepare for bolting into a new day. When Vietnam would twist patriotism into pacifism, and drugs would float from the music of hard-rock into the middle schools, and flower children would pull up their roots and scatter their seed across the land. When there would be demonstrations and sit-ins. For celebration was coming to an end.

Farewell, Happy Days!

Suddenly, without warning, everything changed. CRASH! The plane dashed against the mountain. Bodies bruised. Bones broke. Suddenly, comfort became pain, helplessness diluted power, and prestige became meaningless. With a shock, Friend awoke to a world unknown. Death, the ultimate leveler of persons, hovered. Suddenly, the old assumptions were gone. With a crash—in a flash—gone!

Suddenly, everything changed. CRASH! New values clashed against tradition. Bodies bared. Bonds broke. Suddenly, the permanent became temporary. With a shock, children awoke to adulthood. The death of the planet, the ultimate leveler of countries, hovered—in nuclear disaster, pollution, the depletion of natural resources. Suddenly, nurture, identity, roots were gone. With a crash—in a flash—gone!

The plane slides to a stop on its belly. The crash is over. Dying Father calls to paralyzed

Mother. Unable to move toward each other, to touch, their fingers reach painfully into the cold empty void of distance. Their whispers linger. Confession fills the cabin—not the trimmings— but life itself is the treasure.

The startling drama of the sixties and seventies comes to an end. The tumult is over. Divorce, mobility, anonymity make up the trinity of the new day. Masses cringe in the cold, empty void of physical crowding and psychological isolation. Echoes linger. The masses reach out individually to professionals, paying for structured closeness. Confession fills the time—not the self alone—but relationship is the treasure.

The wings are gone, but the cabin is intact. It is a cache—a storehouse stashed with skis and down jackets, symbols of affluence. A cabin covered by snow, concealed from the world. Suspended in time and space—neither today nor yesterday, neither here nor there. Waiting for rescue. While temperatures drop, and snow buries. Waiting.
The blizzard blankets the cabin windows.

The visions are gone, but the planet is intact. It is a cache-time. A time to horde our resources and stash our possessions. A time to conceal our confusion. Neither achievement nor defeat. Neither "Happy Days" nor demonstrations. Neither yesterday nor tomorrow. Suspended. Waiting for clarity, for direction. While resources deplete, and fresh air fades. Waiting.
Skeletal fingers reach toward the planet.

We are in a time of waiting—a cache-time. A time of storing and sorting. Ours is a day of gentle reprieve—a peaceful postlude to the tumult, and a quiet prelude to the disaster of depletion. The cutting edge—once so clearly visible—eludes us. Causes—once dramatic and flowing in abundance and filled with meaning, rousing a tear in the eye or a battle cry—find us numb, bored, blasé. There is no judgment in this; it is inevitable. We were wounded, and now we withdraw, seeking a sanctuary in which to heal, to recover, to reflect. So we wait.

And we wonder about the recent past and what it meant. We wonder about the future and what it will bring. We wonder about the church. We wonder about ourselves. We wonder about caring—and about courage. How, in a time of hiding, does one know courage, show courage, and grow in courage? Where is courage to be found in a cache-time?

In our confusion, we look outside ourselves. We turn to television and find repetitive sketches of the white-capped heroine of medical stories, the raincoated investigator of detective dramas, the protective collie of animal land. We ask our teen-agers about courage in today's world and find that a typical response is that of a fifteen-year-old boy, who stated with scholarly dignity, "At this time in our history, I see courage as—" Suddenly, his face broke into a grin, "Eating in the school cafeteria!"

Our search does not fill the void and brings a longing for the emphasis placed upon courage by the ancient Greeks, who regarded it as one of the four cardinal virtues. We think of Socrates (470?-399 B.C.), who created a universal and democratic idea of courage, transcending soldierly fortitude with his concept of the courage of wisdom. We think of Plato (427?-347 B.C.), who related courage to the *phylakes* or guardians, the armed aristocracy who represented nobility and grace. We think of Aristotle (384–322 B.C.), who said that the courageous man acts "for what is noble, for that is the aim of virtue," and who, like Plato, saw the soldier as the outstanding example of courage. But we also remember the disintegration of the armed aristocracy, when true courage became separated from soldierly fortitude; for then it converged with wisdom and was defined as the universal knowledge of what is good and evil. As we look at the Greeks, we are not primarily interested in their definitions of courage, but the fact that courage was highly valued by them. This points to one aspect of the void we experience in a cache-time. We feel a lack of courage and long to reclaim this value in our society.

In our search for courage, we turn with hope to public figures, but turn away quickly, disappointed. We recall a time—prior to the seventies—when society's leaders were our heroes and models, our examples of courage lived out. The words of President Franklin Roosevelt echo across the years: "We have nothing to fear but fear itself." He took this statement from the Stoics who made the discovery that the object of fear is fear itself. Epictetus (A.D. 1st-2nd century) stated, "For it is not death or hardship that is a fearful thing, but the fear of death and hardship." The Stoics believed that fear masks all people and things. They felt that if the masks were removed so that the real countenances could be exposed, fear would disappear. Seneca, who lived during the time of Christ, summed this up as: "Nothing is terrible in things except fear itself." These ideas speak to us in a cache-time because masks of fear distort our perception of people and events. We are confused, and we lack clarity.

"Now we see through a glass darkly." Our search leads us to the Bible, where we discover an interesting fact—the words "courage" and "courageous" are rarely used. They occur only fourteen times in the King James and some fifty times in the RSV. Instead of delivering a treatise on the meaning of courage, our Book portrays the essence of courage. Its spirit is poured out on page after page in the witness of our fathers and mothers in the faith; it was embodied by the martyrs in church history; it was exemplified in the life of the One we call Lord.

In our own lives today, we find a few people doing mighty deeds that bring acclaim and make an impact on history. But for most of us, the days pass fairly routinely, with an occasional, unmasked moment when we demonstrate our personal courage. Our small demonstrations may go unnoticed by others—but inside ourselves we know the racing pulse, the knotting stomach, the shaking knees. These demonstrations reflect courage, but the reflection is merely a fragment. Rollo May states: "Courage is not a virtue or value among other personal values like love or fidelity. It is the foundation that underlies and gives reality to all other virtues and personal values."[1] Courage is a pervading attitude in our lives, an undergirding of all that we do, a tumultuous or quiet dimension of who we are. We find courage within ourselves—even in a cache-time.

From this perspective, a consideration of the courage to care becomes multidimensional. We begin with self-awareness, which goes hand in hand with the courage to confess. We move on to self-understanding, which is accompanied by the courage to celebrate. The third dimension is life under God, which calls forth the courage to create. The fourth dimension is life with God, which requires the courage to covenant. It is important to note that this book is not proclaiming *The Answer,* but is struggling with several possibilities. In Hope. Always in hope.

II

The Courage
to Confess

*Midnight approaches. Friend feels the pain in
his back. He huddles closer to Son. Father is
silent. Mother moans. Pilot mumbles, deliri-
ous. The wind howls. It is cold. So cold. Friend
is frightened. So frightened. He is suddenly
aware that what was important this morning,
no longer matters.*

Awareness is the beginning. It is the beginning of
knowing ourselves and others. Awareness arouses
confession because we realize we are not all that we
were created to be. We fall short of our potentialities in
our personal growth and in our relationships with
others. Paul Tillich, who interpreted faith through an
analysis of courage, wrote: "The courage to be is
essentially always the courage to be as a part and the
courage to be as oneself, in interdependence."[1] We
confess our need for greater courage to be as a part and
to be as ourselves.

The Courage to Be as a Part

To borrow a line from Robert Pirsig's *Zen and the
Art of Motorcycle Maintenance,* "We keep passing

unseen through little moments of other people's lives."[2]
We are separated from others, mistrusting, competitive, and anonymous. It is interesting to note that among the psychodynamics and predictive indicators of child abuse are social isolation, transcience, and the lack of a supportive network of relatives or friends; in other words, the parents do not experience being as part—they do not participate in meaningful relationships. One of our contemporary contradictions is that we are always too busy with the mundane or with seeking achievement or with gaining power to build deep and lasting relationships—and yet, it is relationships with others that are of ultimate value. During life we take little time to be authentically involved with others—but at its end, those rare moments are the ones we lift up as cherished. We confess that, although we have a deep need to be a part, we walk through today's world enshrouded in a fog that floats protectively around our life-space, anesthetizing our awareness of those around us.

One dimension of being as part is positively motivated by love and care; together we share growth and pleasure and commitment. But there is also another dimension which is negatively motivated by destructiveness and fear of exclusion; together we are *against* some person or group or race or country. St. Augustine, back in the fourth century, made this confession:

> I would not have committed that theft alone. My pleasure in it was not what I stole but, rather, the act of stealing. Nor would I have enjoyed doing it alone—indeed I would not have done it! O friendship all unfriendly! You strange seducer of the soul, who hungers for mischief from impulses of mirth and wantonness, who craves another's loss without any

desire for one's own profit or revenge—so that, when they say, "Let's go, let's do it," we are ashamed not to be shameless.[3]

The family can be an example of being as part in order to share growth and pleasure and commitment. It is the root of stability in society. The immediate family is a microcosmic reflection of the world family. Awareness of its disintegration brings recognition of the magnitude of our separation from one another. For at the present time, parenting is minimized, divorce divides, and the church looks on in confusion.

Both parents' working full time can contribute to the demise of the family—though this does not have to be the case. The effect depends upon the situation, the strain of the work, the number and ages of the children, and the feasibility of hiring a substitute homemaker. We have moved away from laying a guilt trip on the working mother, but have made the unemployed mother feel defensive about being "just" a homemaker. We have overlooked the importance of this position. A house is where bodies simply appear and disappear; it's just there. A home is more. It is shared by persons who feel a support system and know a family identity. The difference is one of quality, which will not be present if left to chance, but results only from intentional effort and investment of energy by Mother or Father or a substitute. In a home, parents—whether or not they have jobs—invest themselves in parenting, but in a house, parents are content to leave the nurture of their children to peers, siblings, or television. Transactional analysis has taught us that the tapes from our parents are strong, and we unconsciously replay them to our children, who in turn will parent largely as they have been parented. When parents or parental sustitutes are rarely seen—and communed with even less—children's adult models frequently become the characters on TV—that electronic parent that spews violence, over-permissiveness, and materialism across the land. How frightening!

I have struggled with the decision of whether to work outside the home from both sides of the issue. About a decade ago, I took for granted that I would permanently be a full-time homemaker. Our four children were small (the oldest eight), and I was thoroughly enjoying that stage of life—until a seminar speaker called my contentment into question. He encouraged women "to make a contribution to the world." His words still ring in my ears: "It's not enough to come to the end of your life and find that your epitaph reads: She raised three fine sons, who raised three fine sons, who raised three fine sons. That is misuse of time!" I took him seriously and decided to go to graduate school, and then I joined the ranks of the working mother. I aspired toward the epitaph: "She made a contribution to the world—she was an excellent school counselor." At times, however, I was aware of a fear deep inside myself that there might be more to my epitaph: "But in the process, she sacrificed her children, who sacrificed their children, who sacrificed their children." That is timeless misuse!

I began to recognize the absurdity of sacrificing care of the family in order to make "a contribution to the world." In fact, after six years of jolting and shocking real-life experiences with some eighteen hundred students, I became sure that one of the finest contributions a parent can make to the world is rearing one or two fine children, capable of rearing one or two fine children!

I decided to take a sabbatical, giving myself a year for reflection and evaluation. I felt that I had been good at my job as a counselor, knew that I had fully enjoyed it, and recognized that I had grown in my ability to relate with others because of it. However, during my sabbatical, I realized that there was no question in my mind about my family's being better off when I was unemployed. I was not tired, and my mind was not cluttered; I had time to reflect and think and stretch my spirit and be. I was more sensitive and attentive to the individual needs and concerns of my husband and our children. A part of me wanted that sabbatical to turn into retirement. And yet, with four sets of braces and four college educations, that was not very realistic! When the position of Coordinator of Volunteer Services for the Oklahoma City Public Schools opened, I knew there was no job that I would rather have. With ambivalent feelings, I applied for it. The ambivalence increased in intensity when I accepted the position. I was excited about having a channel through which to act upon my commitment to urban public education, and, of course, I appreciated the financial advantages. On the other hand, there was still no question in my mind that not being employed was better for our family's life-style.

To believe that both parents can work full time with no effect upon children is a currently popular delusion. Arlene Cardozo, in *Women at Home,* suggests "that the women's movement has urged wives to follow men in their rush to be gobbled alive by the success ethic, emulating the American man at a time when he has never been less in need of emulation, and more in need of searching his own soul." She says the movement has "deluded women about both the pleasures and the problems of commercial work and about the ease of being a responsible parent and pursuing a career at the same time. (A large part of all work done by men and women is boring and unsatisfying and, as men know well, leaves little enough time for a family or any other form of commitment or self-development.)"[4]

In admitting this to ourselves, we risk the burden of deadening guilt. But if we refuse to allow guilt to hook us, the awareness of difficulties can be positive. It can provide the motivation for at least one parent to invest time and energy in building quality homelife.

Another factor in family disintegration is divorce, which is taking its toll as never before. All marriages have weak stages. It is risky to recognize the warning signals these stages provide, and to untangle the verbal and nonverbal messages—to see and to hear, to become more sensitive, to face the inevitable conflicts which may lead to healthy resolutions (not to be confused with unilateral martyrdom!). During these weak stages, it appears safer to ignore the warning signals and just drift along. To apply another statement from Pirsig:

> Maybe it's not having answers that's defeating both of us. I don't want to go ahead because it doesn't look like any answers ahead. None behind either. Just lateral drift. That's what it is between me and him. Lateral drift, waiting for something.[5]

As we wait, we stagnate in limbo. If we wait long enough, we will reach the point of death in the relationship and eventually divorce—psychologically, if not physically.

As a mother of four, I know how difficult it is to rear children. As a former school counselor, I know that the situation is even more complex for divorced parents—certainly not impossible, but definitely more complex. Divorce in itself does not have to be crippling to children, but the way the situation is handled can be (and in my experience often is) devastating. This one major decision ripples into a thousand others. Bartering begins. Who gets what? Who gets whom? Tension builds. Strain throbs. Parents care a great deal about their children and do not hurt them intentionally, but at this time of painful vulnerability, poor decisions are often made that are unconsciously hurtful. Time and time again parenting accidentally gets caught in the scissor blades that cut a marriage apart. For parents to believe that they can divorce without wounding the child is a delusion. And yet, for them to believe otherwise, often produces guilt, which pointlessly increases the strain and compounds the problem. It is important to move beyond both delusion and guilt. The depth and visibility of the child's scar will be determined by the parents' awareness of the wound and their willingness to heal it. The healing is dependent upon the complex, superhuman efforts of parents, at a time of extreme vulnerability, to maintain the strength to place the needs of the child above their own feelings of hostility, their own instincts and desires. For parents, divorce is a time of breaking apart—and a time of overwhelming need for being a part.

The church as a supportive community is needed by both parties in divorce, and it must be accepting of and caring toward the persons involved. Some of the people I love most in this world (including my mother and father) have been divorced. I've felt their pain and their hurt, and I do not want them to feel that the church judges their lives on the basis of that decision. I want my friends in divorce to experience support and care from the church. But in its eagerness to be broadminded, the church seems to hide from or to apologize for its traditional view of marriage as permanent. Except in situations in which divorce is absolutely necessary (and I dare to suggest that those are rare), the church—if it is to be faithful—has a responsibility to proclaim boldly and without hesitation that its standard is one of lifetime commitment and to follow this proclamation with creative assistance to the partners in resolving rather than escaping their difficulties. The church also has a responsibility to be involved in preventive measures and in marriage enrichment. It has the responsibility to encourage, support, and teach *both* partners in a marriage to refuse to see divorce as an option, or stagnation as an alternative, and to be determined not only to work out problems as they arise, but also to grow as persons and partners and to continually renew and deepen their relationship. The key word, of course, is *both*. A healthy marriage is a full and equal partnerhip—not a unilateral sacrifice. At this time in our history, it is crucial that the church clarify its confusion, that it take a stand against nonessential divorce, but simultaneously, support and care for persons involved in divorce, and that it facilitate growth and commitment in marriage and family life.

The family is in a state of collapse; it is being buried under an accumulation of things and is trodden upon in our hurry to acquire them. We discover that relationships are the real treasure as we grow in the courage to be as part—part of the immediate family, the extended family, the church family, the world family.

The Courage to Be as Oneself

We do not become who we were created to be. We settle for much less. Rather than growing in our awareness of the potentialities God gave us and risking development toward them, we cast ourselves into a common mold, restricting the expression of our inner uniqueness. We hide in the darkness of this confining cocoon, not daring to break forth like a free-floating butterfly—beautiful, colorful, and unique. We confess that we do not have the courage to be as ourselves.

I am Marilyn Brown Oden. What does it mean to be who I am—to be as myself?

The state reduces me to a driver's license number, the city to a street and house number, the phone company to a telephone number, the insurance company to a policy number, the department store to a charge card number, the bank to an account number. Numbers! Numbers! There seems to be no end to them! The computer has erased my name and taken over my identity!

A vision of the future fills my mind. I see myself waiting before the gates of heaven. My eyes scan the puffy clouds for the thin old man in the long white robe sitting at a table, beard flowing to his lap, looking for names in the great Book of Judgment. But he is nowhere in sight. Suddenly, I realize that the process has been updated. Standing in his place beside the pearly gates is a consultant from IBM wearing a Brooks Brothers suit, his hair styled and his nails professionally manicured. His fingers deftly punch the digits of my social security number. And that big computer in the sky spits out the verdict!

I remember a conversation in *The Little Prince:*

Grown-ups love figures. When you tell them that you have made a new friend, they never ask you any questions about essential matters. They never say to you, "What does his voice sound like? What games does he love best? Does he collect butterflies?" Instead, they demand: "How old is he? How many brothers has he? How much does he weigh? How much money does his father make?" Only from these figures do they think they have learned anything about him.[6]

Ouch! Not only do we ask our children these questions, but we also play a numbers game with each other as adults. We demand statistical information that will allow us to categorize each other quickly. We are asking the wrong questions!

Knowing how this game is played and that people all around us are also asking the wrong questions, we certainly don't want to get caught with our numbers down! We invest energy in lengthening our list of accomplishments rather than in deepening our self-awareness. It seems that we are continually reducing the quality of our lives by increasing the quantity of the things we do. We squeeze more and more into our lives, hurrying constantly. We have no time. No time to watch the sun rise or set, to take a quiet little walk. No time to listen to the robins, to touch the shiny new leaves on a tree, to smell the honeysuckle. No time for awareness—to reflect, to think deeply, or to be. No time for the soul to soar in song.

Oblivious to the good in the moment, to discovering who we are, we race after our goals, panting for breath. Pirsig has a different emphasis:

> Plans are deliberately indefinite, more to travel than to arrive anywhere. . . . We want to make good time, but for us now this is measured with emphasis on "good" rather than "time" and when you make that shift in emphasis the whole approach changes.[7]

Each moment provides an opportunity for the soul to sing.

The spirit within has no social security number, is not concerned with statistics, and does not confuse worth with number of achievements. The spirit within cannot be reduced to an ID number. Only as we grow in self-awareness and in the courage to be as ourselves will we discover its expanse.

Fear is a major obstacle to being as part and to being as ourselves. We fear awareness. We fear authenticity. We fear each other. Fear is intensified as our cruelties to one another are headlined in morning papers, pictured in living color on television evening news, and proclaimed every hour, on the hour, by radio. These images which distort our perception of not just one person or one group of persons, are exploitative and become generalized to mankind itself. They mask our real countenances, for images of exploitation far outnumber those of caring for one another. The psychiatrist Willard Gaylin calls our attention to

> the extraordinary capacity of the human being for loving and caring. If there is one fact founded in his biology, essential to his survival and uniquely his own, it is that *Homo sapiens* is a supremely loving animal and a caring one. . . . We survive only by and with caring. This caring nature is a fact of our design, and it is good.[8]

And so, as we confess our alienation and our lack of authenticity, let us do so in constant and grateful awareness of our caring nature. Thanks be to God!

III

The Courage
to Celebrate

*Friend opens his eyes. Dawn! The light of day
descends. The darkness is over! Pain seems to
subside, and groans are subdued. Night has
past! Friend understands—night will come
again, but again, it will also pass away.
Beautiful morning! Oh! Beautiful morning!*

One summer our family went backpacking in the
rugged Colorado Rockies. Six novices ranging from
four to thirty-six years old, we blazed our way through
the wilderness. Silently, as the first, heavy moonless
night crept upon us, the romanticism wore off. We
crowded together in our sleeping bags, strangers
wrapped in blackness, separated from familiar home
ground. Eerie sounds echoed all around as lurking
enemies surrounded us.

Rustling!

    Scratching!

        Plopping!

            Splashing!

                Howling!

                    Scraping!

Gigantic prison walls reached jaggedly into the sky, blocking our escape, while clusters of multi-limbed monsters stood guard. Trembling, we huddled together against these masks which our fear had sculptured in the pervading darkness.

Finally, the first ray of light burst over Bristol Head Mountain, removing the fearful masks and revealing nature's real countenance. The quaking aspens rustled their leaves, accompanying the serenade of the birds. The hungry little chipmunks hurried across the rocks to snatch pieces of crackers, their claws scratching as they scurried. Trout surfaced and then dived with a plop into the clear blue lake that narrowed into a winding, splashing stream. A wolf howled his loneliness from a ridge across the canyon, and a deer, leaping gracefully through the forest, stopped suddenly to scrape his sprouting antlers. Stretching into the sky, snow-capped peaks encircled us, and magnificent green spruce trees clustered nearby.

We walked across the carpet of sparkling dew and gathered wood to build a fire. We shared its warmth, smiling at one another and laughing at our fear during the night. Deeply, we congratulated ourselves on surviving undefeated. We knew darkness would descend again, but we committed ourselves to continue our journey through the mountains. We lifted our mugs of coffee and hot chocolate, celebrating the darkness and the light.

As human beings we journey on through life, through the darkness of despair and the light of love. As Christians, we seek the courage to celebrate life in its totality—the whole pilgrimage—glowing through the light stages and growing through the dark ones, living a life that is a song of celebration, a life that praises God for both beauty and ugliness, for both dreams and depressions, for both kindness and cruelty. *For all of life is in God's hands.* This is our ultimate understanding; it is the foundation of our celebration. To live a life with this understanding is to celebrate each moment we live in the present—in the now—and to celebrate presence in each moment we live.

The celebrative life lives fully in the present—continually greeting each new moment as it arrives. If we look wistfully backward as it passes, we miss the opportunity to greet the next new moment. Likewise, if we focus on the future, we stumble unseeingly over the constantly unfolding present. Pirsig tells us:

> We're in such a hurry most of the time we never get much chance to talk. The result is a kind of endless day-to-day shallowness, a monotony that leaves a person wondering years later where all the time went and sorry that it's all gone.[1]

But how difficult it is to live in the present!

We can visit any neighborhood and find people demonstrating their resistance to the present. Walk with me down my street, and I'll show you what I mean.

Across the street in the house with the pretty plants growing in the front window is Aunt Polly, a lovely lady living in the past. She always calls on new parents in the neighborhood when their baby arrives, and takes them a handmade quilt pieced together with leftover scraps from the sewing she did for her children and grandchildren. She tells each mother how much the new baby looks like her own first child and how fast children grow up and go away. Invariably, when guests come to visit, she invites them to walk down her long hall, which is a wall-to-wall gallery of family portraits. She talks about each one and then begins the second part of the ritual—looking through her family albums. She repeats the ritual time and time again. Her yesterdays fill each today.

Next door in the white house with the red shutters is Susan. I can remember when I first met her some time ago. She felt set apart—perhaps above—as one of the faithful few. She touched the needy at every turn and then waited for her reward. But, to her chagrin, the result was not the stars she was expecting, but the scars of her involvement. Now embittered and filled with cynicism, most afternoons she escapes by playing bridge; other days, she just drinks away. One meaningless moment follows another, paralyzing the possibilities of the present.

The Fowlers live in the large brick house; they are a couple in their forties. He rushed toward the top like a racehorse wearing blinders. He has spent the last two decades living for the future. It's a habit now. A traumatic habit—for when one reaches midlife, there is a jolting awareness that suddenly the future has arrived in the present. Look. He's coming out to get the morning paper; he always reads the stock market reports. Even this early in the morning he's as immaculate as his manicured lawn! But look closely. See his jaw tight with strain? His white knuckles as he

clutches his Bloody Mary? Listen! He's mumbling
something:

> I find myself consumed
> Consumed by the games that I play
> Consumed! No time!
> No time to be alone
> > to think
> > to look inside myself
> Facade! Facade!
> Display the proper face!
> A harried pace
> A constant race
> I drive myself. Drive myself
> Drive
> > Drive
> > > Driven!

His tomorrow consumes each today.
  Pirsig suggests:

> Mountains should be climbed with as little effort as
> possible and without desire. . . . Then, when you're no
> longer thinking ahead, each footstep isn't just a means
> to an end but a unique event in itself. *This* leaf has
> jagged edges. *This* rock looks loose. From *this* place
> the snow is less visible, even though closer. These are
> things you should notice anyway. To live only for some
> future goal is shallow. *It's the sides of the mountain
> which sustain life, not the top. Here's* where things
> grow.[2] (Italics in last 2 sentences are mine.)

Common to every neighborhood are those who do not
live in the present—the past-oriented Aunt Pollys, the
cynical Susans, and the future-oriented Fowlers. How
difficult it is to *live* in the present!
  But the celebrative life does this. It sees the top of
the mountain and accepts it as a destination. But there
is no desire to be catapulted from here to there. The

pilgrimage itself is seen as important—being sensitive to each leaf and rock along the way. If our pilgrimage teaches us nothing else, we learn that light follows darkness—that living leads to dying, and that in the midst of death, new life can be created. The celebrative life fully experiences the joy and the pain, the light and the darkness in the present.

Just as the life of celebration celebrates each moment we live in the present, it also celebrates presence in each moment we live. Paul Tillich tells us that each person is unique, unrepeatable, irreplaceable, and unexchangeable.[3] At times each of us needs to be present to the self. To be alone—not as an escape, in a dull, numb kind of limbo—but for self-awareness, reflection, evaluation, and appreciation. How difficult it is for us to be present to ourselves!

At times each of us needs the presence of another—to see *us,* to hear us, to touch us. The other also needs this same presence from us. Presence is more than just being together physically. It is being together in full personhood. We can tell when the other is giving us the old familiar nod, pretending to listen while mentally floating off someplace else. We know that we do this to others also. We tend to delude ourselves, however, that we are so skilled in the technique of nonlistening that they believe we are listening! We waste many unrepeateable moments of our lives being together physically—but not fully *present.* How difficult it is for us to share presence with one another!

When we are threatened, the need for presence is overwhelming. For example, to children the word "divorce" is a scary monster that thunders through the front door and invades the security of home. Mother and father, in a state of upheaval and understandably consumed by their own trauma, are unable to be fully present to the child. At the same time, admitting separation is difficult and painful, and many parents, wanting to avoid gossip (partially in order to protect their children), restrict them to secrecy. Children are expected to experience alone the volcanic eruptions of their parents' dying marriage and stand in silent isolation during the earthquaking nest-shaking tremors dividing the home.

The lack of presence within today's families troubled me repeatedly as a middle-school counselor. Let me illustrate by sharing a situation that is becoming more and more typical. We'll call the student Sara. For some time she had walked alone through the darkness of night, stumbling over the obstacles of her crumbling world. Finally, she came to my office.

Sara glanced at me and looked away. Her face, framed by pretty red curls, was thin and drawn, and there were dark circles under her eyes. As she sat—so small in the chair—she unconsciously picked at the quick around her thumbnail. It was raw and sore.

Her eyes toured the walls of my office, stopping at each poster. She glanced at me again and started to say something, but stopped and lowered her eyes, picking nervously at her thumb.

"Which poster do you like, Sara?" I asked.

"That one." She pointed to the one behind my desk that showed a chicken hatching from its shell, looking around at the world, and then closing himself back into his shell.

"I like that one, too." I smiled at her. "Some days are like that."

She peered at me suspiciously, intently. Then she took a deep breath. "You can't tell anybody anything I tell you, right." It was more a statement than a question.

I nodded.

"Not teachers or the other kids."

I nodded again.

She sat up straight, her hazel eyes piercing through mine. "Not even parents?" This time it was a question—a vital one.

"No, Sara. I wouldn't tell your parents anything we talk about—unless you and I decide together that it would be the best thing to do."

Her face loosened somewhat, and she looked away from me. "My mother made me promise not to tell." Then her eyes met mine again, uncertain. "I've never broken a promise to her before."

"You're worried about breaking a promise to your mother, Sara." She nodded as I continued. "And you also feel worried about something else." She nodded again.

Her eyes were beginning to tear. Her little face worn, her voice tight, she whispered brokenly, sadly, "Mother and Daddy . . . are getting . . . a . . . divorce." She shuddered as she said "divorce."

Then, she slowly exhaled as if releasing air from a swollen balloon. It was as though in the process of merely saying these words, a great weight was being lifted from her tiny shoulders.

But the relief was only temporary. Another burden replaced the former—the burden of guilt from a broken promise. "You mustn't tell." She was scared.

"It's all right, Sara. I won't. This is a safe place to talk."

"I didn't want to tell anyone. I tried not to. But it's all I've thought about."

"The divorce just stays on your mind." I said softly.

She nodded. The war between the parents had been waged, and Sara was sworn to secrecy. "The other night I stayed all night with my friend. Her mother asked me how my parents were. And I thought for a minute she knew. But she didn't. She was just being polite. And then my friend and I went to bed, and it was dark, and we were talking. Oh, it was so hard not to tell. I'm always thinking about it. I thought maybe if I just told her, and if she promised not to tell. But she might tell just one friend, and her friend might tell someone. And pretty soon it'd be all over school. And then my mother would find out I'd told."

Sara was talking as fast she she could, pouring out her bottled up feelings. "Every night I've been having trouble going to sleep. I just lie in bed, and the tears roll down my face. No one hears me. Daddy hasn't moved out yet. They're just getting ready to work all that out. And I'm afraid when I wake up some morning he'll be gone. That night I stayed with my friend, I wanted to come back home. I was afraid he'd leave, and I wouldn't even be home. It was awful. I was just lying there crying—almost all night. Afraid my friend would hear me and wonder why. But she didn't wake up. I'm not going to stay all night with anyone ever again."

She paused a minute to catch her breath. "It feels so good to be able to talk about all this." She had stopped picking her thumb.

"I'm sure your mother didn't realize how much she was expecting when she asked for that promise."

She nodded. "But I kept it. Until today. But telling you is like—it's like telling nobody."

I smiled inside myself.

"I wish I knew why they don't want to stay married. Maybe if I'd been better—if I'd helped more—if I'd been neater—if I hadn't done so many things wrong —maybe they wouldn't even want a divorce then." She dug into the quick of her thumb. Guilt had surfaced again—the guilt echoed in so many children because they fear they have somehow caused their parents' divorce and therefore, should also be able to figure out how to fix it. Her thumb was bleeding. "They get so *mad* at each other." Sobbing, she picked up the box of Kleenex on the table and held it tight to her chest. I sat close beside her.

Sara's Mother. At one time Sara's mother had seen herself as a dutiful wife and a doting mother. Her husband had taken her for granted, and so had their children. Her maintenance of the household had been assumed rather than appreciated. She was tired of feeling bound to buzzers—if not the oven, the dryer. She found herself bored with more and more time on her hands. And beneath it all, more and more alone. She was present to her family, but did not feel their presence in return. She decided to take a job.

Abruptly, her life changed. She not only experienced appreciation from her colleagues, but also felt as successful in her work as her husband was in his. His support and a word of congratulation would have meant a great deal to her. Instead, she received only condemnation for the undone housework, which was continually waiting for her. In the beginning she had hoped that he would help her; now she realized that he never would. The more criticism she received at home, the more she focused on her job. In time her job, not her family, became the center of her life.

Sara's mother did not like the idea, but divorce seemed necessary. She knew she could not go back to the way it had been, to the void—the lack of presence —she had experienced before. That chapter of her life was closed forever.

Sara's Father. Sara's father had always worked very hard to provide for his family. He was proud of what he had done for them. He felt that he sacrificed himself daily on their behalf and asked very little in return—a good dinner, clean clothes, and a feeling that they appreciated him.

His wife used to ask about his job and how his day had gone—to be present to him. Not anymore. Instead of showing interest in *his* work, she just talked about *hers.* She used to be the bridge between him and their children—this too had ceased. Now he had to communicate with them by himself, and he didn't know how. They were strangers.

What a void he felt! Estranged from his wife. Estranged from his children. He was in the way. Uncared for. Alone. Lonely. He did not like the idea, but divorce seemed necessary. He knew that he could not endure life this way—living with his family, yet feeling isolated from them. Everything had changed— and he could not.

Finally, Sara stopped crying. We talked a while longer, and then she was ready to leave. She set the box of Kleenex back down on the table. "Thank you," she said. "I was like a balloon about to pop."

"I'm glad we could talk, Sara. We can't solve the problem, but we can talk about your feelings anytime you'd like." I put my arm around her small thin shoulders as she stepped toward the door. "Your mother and daddy are lucky to have you for a daughter." Her eyes were still red, but a smile crossed her tired little face.

And Sara went on to class with teachers and students unaware of her turmoil. She went on to language arts to be in a play, on to math to take a test. But the real drama was going on within her family. And the real test was going on within herself. I watched her walk away, hoping she would pass it.

Presence—needed—yet mistrusted, hesistantly requested, and rarely given. Left, with more and more frequency, to the professionals.

Seeking presence, we come together in communities of various types, shapes, and sizes. Tillich reminds us of the significance of each unique person in making up the total membership of a community. "A part of a whole is not identical with the whole to which it belongs. But the whole is what it is only with the part."[4]

Each person, in a worship service, a task force, a church school class, is a part of that particular group, and the group would not be what it is without that specific, unexchangeable, individual member.

Let's look again at my neighborhood. It is what it is because of Aunt Polly and Susan and Mr. Fowler—and even me. The transfer or death of any one of us would cause it to be changed, never again to be quite the same.

But even within one's neighborhood there are masks of fear, and they grow in number and intensity as we expand the size of the community. Let's look at the city as viewed by Pirsig:

> The city closes in on him now, . . . Form and substance without Quality. That is the soul of this place. Blind, huge, sinister and inhuman: seen by the light of fire flaring upward in the night from the blast furnaces in the south, through heavy coal smoke deeper

and denser into the neon of BEER and PIZZA and LAUNDROMAT signs and unknown and meaningless signs along meaningless straight streets going off into other straight streets forever. . . .

Along the streets . . . he can never see anything through the concrete and brick and neon but he knows that buried within it are grotesque, twisted souls forever trying the manners that will convince themselves they possess Quality, learning strange poses of style and glamour vended by dream magazines and other mass media, . . . [5]

We stand in the darkness, separated by our anonymity. We do not know. We are not known. We hide behind our masks. We tremble. We peek out in fear.

Suddenly, we realize that other eyes are also peering out. But still we hide—alone—aware that each pair of eyes perceives the view in a different way. Each of us distorts in the darkness, for we see different shapes in the shadows. Fear of reality deters us from shining a flood light on the view because we are not ready for the revelation of countenances that would confuse our belief systems or weaken our prejudices.

An experiment with college students conducted during Franklin Roosevelt's presidency demonstrates our distortion in perception. Young Republicans and Democrats heard a speech containing an equal number of favorable and critical statements about the New Deal program. When tested afterward, each party felt the speech had supported its view and recalled the appropriate quotes. [6] In addition to sifting out information that will support our beliefs, we also tend to recall evidence that favors our viewpoint and forget evidence that is contrary to it. Retested two weeks later, the same college students revealed increased differences in remembered content—each had enhanced his bias. [7]

When we try to conceive of the world as community,

we find ourselves divided into a massive international jigsaw puzzle, where each nation peeks at the others from behind a mask of fear. Our various perceptions lead to misunderstndings, and our misunderstandings lead to conflict—which can be creative or destructive. When conflict between nations is not only destructive but is also carried to the extreme, we risk war—with nuclear weapons already stockpiled! One frightening variable in whether or not international conflict leads to war seems to be the personalities of the leaders involved. Northwestern University made a study based on the events and personalities that led to the outbreak of World War I. There were two groups of simulation teams: one matched the personalities of the leaders who made the major decisions in the 1914 crisis; the other group consisted of personality types that differed from the leaders. The two groups received camouflaged historical messages so that items revealing the particular crisis would be suitably masked. In this study a significant similarity emerged between the decisions of the real leaders in 1914 and their psychologically matched simulation teams; the decisions of both led to war. Conversely, the nonmatched teams found other ways to handle their conflicts; they negotiated, called a conference, and avoided war.[8] Today we need leaders who see the planet as a world community, who have the courage to live together under conditions of multicultural diversity and limited space and resources, and who think as global men and women. Malachi Martin, in *Three Popes and the Cardinal,* makes our position clear.

> The most important and inescapable fact about men . . . is that all men, wherever and whenever they existed, exist, and will exist, belong to a "human

family." . . . It is the family men constitute because each man shares with every other man the equality of being human and the dignity of equal human rights. . . .

There is manifest, only in our modern day, the beginning of a unity among men which was never achieved before in human history. . . . It is merely and poignantly a community of increasingly pressing needs. Men today are truly interdependent as never before.[9]

We are truly interdependent as nations, cities, neighborhoods, individuals—as never before. And yet we hide in fear behind our masks—as always before.

As we live our lives, we backpack up the mountain through the light and the darkness, aware each step of the way of the weight of the many burdens carried in our packs. At times we focus on the top—on our future arrival—ignoring the leaves and the rocks as we go. At times we look back, seeing only where we have been. At times we give up, take off our packs, and sit down—badly in need of presence and the Presence. But there are also times when we see—really see—those sitting beside the trail and make ourselves present to their needs. Pirsig speaks to the meaning of presence:

I work off the resentment at having to do this [carry both his pack and mine in relays] by realizing that it isn't any more work for me, actually, than the other way. It's more work in terms of reaching the top of the mountain, but that's only the nominal goal. In terms of the real goal, putting in good minutes, one after the other, it comes out the same; in fact, better.[10]

Saying a continually renewed *yes* to the journey as well as to the destination is to live out our understanding that *all* of life is in God's hands. To be aware of each rock and each leaf beside the trail, to appreciate each Aunt Polly and Susan and Mr. Fowler, to be sensitive to each Sara along the way, to be willing to carry the pack of another, is to have the courage to celebrate each moment we live in the present and to celebrate presence in each moment we live.

IV

The Courage
to Create

*A moment of clarity comes to Pilot. He takes
charge: Someone must go for help. Find a
stream. Follow it down. Our only hope
. . . Go . . . Down . . . Pilot drifts off again into
delirium.*

*Friend moves to the cabin door and forces it
open, wincing at the pain in his back. He looks
out at the incredible white vastness. Impossible! He shakes his head. Totally impossible!*

The Judeo-Christian story tells us that God blew on
dust, and man was created. Our vision is not clear but
cluttered, and our faith is not whole but fragmented.
And yet, here we are—dust with dreams.

A friend of mine told me about six children who had
been born into extreme poverty. They grew up in a
dirt-floor hovel down by the river in the worst poverty
area of Oklahoma City. Their clothes were worn over
and over again, until they were threadbare, patched,
and the patches became threadbare. Shoes were saved
for winter use only, and outgrown ones were passed
down the line from child to child. By the time a pair

reached the youngest, water sloshed in through the holes in the soles. They awoke each morning with hungry stomachs—and an empty cupboard. Six children—poor, hungry, and fatherless—with a mother who loved music. Absurdity of absurdities, she somehow managed to buy two season tickets to the symphony every year. She took one child with her to each performance, passing down the turns just as she did the shoes. She took them singly—hungry and barely clothed—to art museums and exhibits. Amazingly, she also found money for the theater, and each child went with her to one play a year. The six children grew up in their one-room hovel, padding across the dirt floor with bare feet, wearing worn-out clothes, expecting to be hungry—but taking the arts for granted.

My friend, who had recently completed her doctoral work, continued her story. "The older five grew up to be exceptionally creative. One is a successful artist. Another is an architect who's received awards for his outstanding work. And not a one lives down by the river."

"What happened to the youngest?" I asked.

"Well," she smiled with a twinkle in her warm brown eyes, "I'll never forget sloshing down the road on a wet blustery day, with mud oozing in through the holes of my shoe soles—happily on the way to the symphony hand in hand with my mother."

Dust with dreams. That is the magic. Those six children grew up victims of hunger but not of hopelessness, of poverty but not of powerlessness. Their mother dreamed of a different way. As long as we have a dream, we have hope. And as long as we have hope, there is a *possibility* that we can create the dream.

The children by the river were products of the depression. Perhaps it is harder to dream in our cache-time. Problems have not been solved, but their symptoms are less obvious, and our blindness to them is comfortable. Recently, some friends who had been part of the hip culture at its peak observed that college students today do not have a cause—there is nothing they really care about. Later, some friends in their midyears expressed confusion in that a few years ago we were in the forefront and felt clear about the cutting edge, but now none of us seems even to know where the cutting edge is. Martin Marty refers to our time as a "settled-down time."[1] We have been through a time of storming toward our dreams; now, we wait, catching our breath, sitting in the cache in confused calm.

Alves sketches our situation:

> The past two decades have been the years when we were expelled from paradise. Our innocence was lost. We had been brought up carefully protected by the illusions past generations had created. . . .
>
> Hollywood created such deep habitual ruts of thought in the American mind that one came to assume as a matter of course that every tragedy had a happy ending. . . . And then, one after another, [our illusions] fell from their pedestals. . . .
>
> We saw with horror that our affluence and comfort were built upon violence, genocide, earlier slavery, and exploitation and greed. And with this discovery came the vision that the world must and could be transformed, and that this was the task of our generation to carry through. . . .
>
> But [these] hopes were never fulfilled.[2]

He suggests that there followed an intolerable, excruciating realization of the chasm separating what existed from what had been envisioned, and that to alleviate our pain, we adjusted. The magic of adjustment is compelling because it makes us happy by erasing our awareness of the problem. We translate "action is no longer possible" into "action is no longer necessary." We save ourselves from pain by becoming insensitive. We are no longer seekers, for we have nothing to find. We adapt ourselves to a dreamless acceptance of what exists. We become resigned. Alves compares us with ducks:

> Once we were like wild ducks, beating our wings, flying high up in the skies, facing danger and fatigue—permanent emigrants, always moving from one place to another. But then we looked down and saw a flock of happy, fat domestic ducks, and we envied them. We joined them and became as they are.[3]

Later he asks, since we are now "too fat to fly, why go on ludicrously flapping [our] wings? It is easier to put on the identity of the domestic duck."[4] It is easier to adjust—to let resignation write the obituary to our dreams.

Or, to withdraw from the real world which is easier than struggling to create a new way within the world. Throughout history, people from all walks of life have chosen to withdraw from the world. Saints built monasteries, the counterculture moved into communes, and sensitive people of all kinds convinced themselves that their dreams were delicate blossoms unable to survive among the scorpions of the human desert. So they planted the seeds of their dreams in greenhouses, away and apart from the world. They lived a gospel of refuge and reclusion.

But this is not the gospel of Jesus Christ. He was not a recluse, drawing apart from his culture, escaping from conflict. He ate and breathed and walked and healed and taught and loved and lived in the world, creating a new way that ultimately took him to the cross. We want courage without suffering; we want birth without labor; we want resurrection without the cross. Illusions and fantasies can occur away and apart from the world of reality, but dreams are enacted in tension with the world.

America's first black poetess knew that tension. She knew the terror of being kidnapped as a little girl, the horror of the voyage on the slave ship from Senegal to Boston, the atrocity of being sold. A *nameless* beginning! Called Phillis by her master, John Wheatley, she learned quickly, created poetry, became a Christian, and joined Old South Church. At twenty, she published her first volume of poetry, visited London, was entertained by lords and ladies, received Milton's *Paradise Lost* from the Lord Mayor, and was to be presented at court. She touched the lives of King George III and John Hancock, was admired by George Washington, and her second volume of poetry was to be dedicated to Benjamin Franklin. At the death of her owner, she became a freed woman, married John Peters, and had three children.

Her financial benefactors were lost, due to the cost of the Revolutionary War; her second volume of poetry was never published; and her treasured Milton was sold in payment of her husband's debts. (It was later donated to the Harvard Library). She came to live in a cheap boarding house. She scrubbed floors until her fragile health broke and then could afford no wood to warm her room and no food to feed her only living child. Her dreams ended in drudgery, darkness, and finally death. Phillis Wheatley Peters—prodigy in poetry —died on Sunday, December 5, 1784, at the age of thirty-one. She and her child were buried together in an unmarked grave. A *nameless* ending!

A study of her life brings rage and tears and admiration. She did not withdraw into the greenhouse of her mind, choosing a life of fantasy and illusion; she remained in tension with the world of reality. Nor did she sacrifice her dreams; she maintained the courage to continue struggling toward them to the end of her tragic life.

All creative acts are dependent upon a dream and upon the courage to struggle toward that dream. In a creative act we dare to form from the nonexistent something that exists—to make being of nonbeing. It requires a concentrated encounter of all that we are with that which we envision. It demands from us the courage to risk ourselves in making our vision a reality. A creative act may end in a poem, a novel, a painting, a song; it may end in a fresh dimension within our individual community of faith or a new social order. It may take hours or years or generations. And there is no assurance that the dream will ever be attained; and even if it is, there is no guarantee of extrinsic reward.

So it is with the life under God. To choose to live life under God depends upon a dream—a dream of living and loving as Christ lived and loved—and upon the courage to struggle to create that dream. The life under God does not resign itself to the ways of the world, adapting to materialism, superficiality, hedonism; it dares to keep its dreams in focus and to soar toward them. The life under God does not hide in seclusion from the world; it serves within it. Nor does it waste itself *reacting;* it is too busy *acting* the word of love. It does not try to usurp another's power, but lives the stance of Christ—that the power of love is greater than the love of power. To choose life under God, from a Christian perspective, requires that the whole self—all that one is—encounter Jesus Christ as model and messiah. In doing so one hears the word—the creative word—that comforts the troubled and troubles the comfortable. For Jesus Christ was not a mystic that meditated thirty-three years in the wilderness; he was not a charismatic, hiding behind a mask of glossolalia; he was not a critical observer, standing apart and shaking his head. He was a participant in the world of reality, living life under God, courageously struggling to create a new way.

Choosing to live under God calls for the courage to commit ourselves to bring the dream of a more Christ-like world to fruition. We are called to this lifelong struggle, recognizing that there is no guarantee that the struggle will be extrinsically rewarding. In fact, we risk crucifixion—and we do so for an unattainable dream. How much easier it would be to give up—to become a domestic duck. Listen to Dory Previn:

> i can't go on
> i mean
> i can't go on
> i really
> can't go on
> i swear
> i can't go on
>
> so
> i guess
> i'll get up
> and go on.[5]

That is the life under God. One gets up and goes on. One refuses to be a domestic duck. The life under God has the faith enacted by the hummingbird. Scientifically, that little bird cannot complete its migration; it is physically impossible for it to make the flight from beginning to end. Yet, in the face of powerlessness, the hummingbird faithfully soars through the air year after year, defying the laws of science. In the face of powerlessness, the life under God dares to dream of justice, equality, honor, and beauty, and refuses to allow these impossible dreams to die.

According to Alves, what B. F. Skinner's behaviorism has demonstrated for us is that people *may* behave like animals.[6] An animal feels pain and avoids it. Man feels pain, but asks if he can change the situation. If he is totally void of creative possibilities and absolutely without hope of transforming the situation, if he cannot refuse to play the game nor change the rules, if there is no way out—then he will follow the logic of pain and pleasure and learn the "right" answers, like a rat in a Skinner box. It is important for us to acknowledge, however, that we have a remarkable ability to withstand pain as long as we believe in our values—as long as we preserve hope.

Remember the mother who lived down by the river.

Remember Viktor Frankl who survived Auschwitz and wrote *Man's Search for Meaning.*

Remember Kunta Kinte in *Roots,* who dreamed of freedom, and kept his dream alive generation after generation.

Remember Jeremiah. Jerusalem was under siege, deliverance seemed impossible, no one could plan for the future—and Jeremiah bought a piece of land. That act symbolized his hopes: "The time will come when houses, fields, and vineyards will again be bought and sold in this land" (Jer. 32:15). Jeremiah refused to take refuge from the world. Nor was he a reactionary, for he rejected the revolutionaries' illusions. And neither was he resigned, a priest of the status quo, filled with despair and lacking a vision of the future. Although in captivity, he kept his dream alive.

Powerlessness is never hopelessness as long as the dream of a better way remains alive. As long as there is hope, there is the possibility of the dream becoming a reality. And as we reach toward that dream, we stretch and grow, and our boundaries of love and joy and freedom and responsibility enlarge. For as Christians we follow a Man—a creative man—whose life brought his death and whose death brought us life.

Thoreau affirms dreams:

> I learned this, at least, by my experiment: that if one advances confidently in the direction of his dreams, and endeavors to live the life which he has imagined, he will meet with a success unexpected in common hours. . . . If you have built castles in the air, your work need not be lost; that is where they should be. Now put the foundations under them.

We are dust with dreams—daring in a time of waiting to keep the spark of our dreams alive.

V

The Courage
to Covenant

Friend looks from person to person—lost and lonely, cold and hungry, suffering together, prisoners of the cache. Father's silence is eternal. Mother, too, is silent, still. Son takes her hand in his. Tears flow from her closed eyes. Pilot mumbles deliriously. These few against the cosmos. They are covenanted together—not in word, but in spirit.

To move from life *under* God to life *with* God requires the courage to covenant. When I think of the courage to covenant, I think of planting a date tree. As the saying goes, "He who plants dates will not eat them." Now radishes—that's another matter; it's only a few weeks from the planting to the picking. Ours is a time of eating from the date trees planted by our ancestors and of planting radishes for ourselves; a time that is void of permanence and fearful of intimacy; a time when we worship the new and blow about like tumbleweeds on the surface of the earth, unrooted and rootless. A covenant requires the courage to refuse to play that game; it requires the courage to make commitments of depth—to plant a date tree in a time when others are planting radishes.

The word "covenant" is outmoded in our culture. It got lost some place in the maze of our changing beliefs. Today, it is assumed that love is temporary, that the loved one is replaceable, and that pleasure is a product we can purchase. We begin to pass this assumption along to our children when they are small. There are many teachers—the toy manufacturers, for example. What are children learning when a toy company announces that a new, improved, and prettier doll can be obtained by trading in an old one? Think about that. It does not matter that something old is loved and has been long valued. All that matters is that it can be exchanged for something new. The Skin Horse in *The Velveteen Rabbit* sends us a relevant message:

> Generally, by the time you are Real, most of your hair has been loved off, and your eyes drop out and you get loose in the joints and very shabby. But these things don't matter at all, because . . . you can't be ugly, except to people who don't understand.[1]

We live in a world filled with people who don't understand. I find a great deal of similarity between a child's trading in an old used doll for a new improved model, and an adult's trading in the old spouse for a better looking one!

But toy manufacturers are not the only teachers. Think what parents often do when a pet dies. I remember when Danna Lee our daughter was three, and our dog was killed. I didn't want her to be upset, to cry, to experience the pain of grief and loss. I wanted to fix things for her by quickly getting her another dog. Bill strongly disagreed. "Marilyn," he argued, "one life can't replace another. Not with pets, nor people. You can't buy a substitute for the loved." Many times since that moment long ago I have been grateful for his wisdom.

Another area in which our culture seems confused is in its emphasis on pleasure as a commercial commodity. Long ago, Nez Perces Indian children learned the tragedy of greed and the virtue of honor from their elders and through tribal legends. Today, I fear American children are learning the tragedy of honor and the virtue of greed from their adult models and through television life-styles. Alves calls attention to the exploitation of pleasure as a commercial commodity:

> Emotional experiences become goods. They are sold like bubble gum and dog food—"as if they were things." The spiritualization of economy is nothing more than the final reduction of the spirit to the condition of canned food. Within the superindustrial society there is only one means of appropriation left: that of buying.[2]

It is as if all our senses are being consumed by one new sense—the sense of *having*. The joys of experiencing and remembering are made to appear insufficient. The miracle of seeing is diminished, for it is not until the splendorous view of Uncompaghre Mountain is reproduced on canvas and hung above the mantel that the sense of having is fulfilled. The miracle of touching is diminished, for it is not until the aged piece of beautiful knotted, weathered wood is dragged down from the mountainside and carefully transported home that the sense of having is fulfilled. The miracle of smelling is diminished, for it is not until the wild rose is transplanted to our own backyard that the sense of having is fulfilled. The miracle of hearing is diminished, for it is not until Beethoven's Fifth Symphony played by Leonard Bernstein and the New York Philharmonic Orchestra is recorded and purchased for our own stereo that the sense of having is fulfilled. The miracle of tasting is diminished, for it is not until the crêpes of the French restaurant can be duplicated in our own special crêpes cookware that the sense of having is fulfilled.

But what of the person whose sense of having *is* fulfilled—and who still feels empty? What of the person who becomes an alcoholic or commits suicide? Why does that happen? Perhaps because it is not possible to equate economic well being—*having*—with happiness, human fulfillment, and meaning in life. We do not live by bread alone. How long ago we were told that, yet we still haven't learned it. If there is a secret to finding meaing in life, I think I know what it is. It is not to be found in the popular hedonistic principle of *getting* all that we can, but in the rare Christian principle of *giving* all that we can.

We have allowed ourselves to become twisted into anonymous, mass-produced pawns who buy into absurd cultural games without questioning their validity or rules. Alves describes Jesus as looking at the cultural game of his day—at the tradition and the law that had been converted into a game of human hyprocrisy—and simply refusing to play it. A task before us as Christians is to have the courage to stand in the midst of our world and dare to refuse to play such games. Instead of skimming the surface in a shallow, greedy, selfish, meaningless existence, to dare to covenant one with another, to struggle toward depth and honor and self-giving and meaning—to plant a date tree in our life-space.

One of the best ways to understand the concept of covenant is to see it in terms of marriage (admittedly, marriage is becoming a shakier illustration of covenant every day). Robert Weiss, author of *Marital Separation,* says that we have desacralized marriage. He does not attribute this trend primarily to easier divorce laws and sexual permissiveness, but to the intensity of our impatience with any barriers to self-realization. "To a greater extent than seems true elsewhere in the world, we Americans seem to cherish our right to the unimpeded pursuit of happiness no matter how much sorrow that pursuit may engender."[3] Roman Catholic philosopher-writer Michael Novak adds that our highest moral principle is flexibility and that we view life as solitary and brief and see its purpose as self-fulfillment. "In such a vision of the self, marriage is merely an alliance. . . . They say of marriage that it is deadening, when what they mean is that it drives us beyond adolescent fantasies and romantic dreams."[4] Benjamen DeMott sums up our new stance as scrapping "in sickness and in health" for "I do my thing and you do your thing."[5] Today, we seem to be justifying the existence of the impermanent. Why not rip the date tree out of the ground and plant the radish seed in its place? Why not be rid of the old, when we can supplant it quickly with the new—a fresh salad or a fresh spouse—it doesn't seem to make much difference! Remember Huxley in *Brave New World:* "Ending is better than mending."[6] Why not trade in that old doll today.

But I want to move on to the idealistic. Let me share my dream—a dream of a creative covenant in marriage, where divorce is not an option to either partner, but likewise, neither is just keeping-it-together stagnation.

I dream of translating the wedding vows into a creative covenant. It is a dream that moves beyond a marriage contract, beyond the promise to live together until the intervention of death. I dream of a husband

and a wife covenanting to climb life's mountains freely fettered together.

The fetters are not like chains of clanking iron. But elongated rubberbands, soft and elastic. No key. No lock. Fetters retained by choice because the covenant is renewed. Or removed by choice—and the covenant broken. Freely fettered as in a three-legged race, husband and wife begin their climb—their stumbling struggle, their journey of joy.

Awkward and clumsy in their first few steps, they discover the need for a common cadence, a flexible pace. Not his cadence, nor hers. Not her pace, nor his—but theirs.

Wife is attracted by a flower and stops to study it, to accept the gift of its beauty, to experience the potential of the moment. Husband, uninterested, moves on. The fetters stretch, accommodating their distance. But if she continues to linger, and he to proceed, the fetters are stretched taut, and the limits reached. She must decide to continue with her husband, leaving the flower behind, or, to choose the flower, ceasing her climb—or she may decide to bring that flower with her into her marriage. And he must decide to continue on without her, to be content to cease his climb—or to support her in bringing this new interest into their marriage.

Soon, he is captivated by a flower that does not attract her. Again the fetters stretch, and again each must decide.

There will be many flowers, many stops, many decisions. And the couple will overcome—or be defeated by—jealousy, impatience, possessiveness. For some the climb will cease, and for others the fetters will be removed—but there are those whose journey together will continue, and it will be a colorful one,

---

enriched by broadened interests and mutual support and the joy of growth.

But then one day the husband suddenly wants to study one flower and the wife another. Simultaneously. In opposite directions. Their fetters prohibit conflicting pursuits. Dramatic dialogue ensues:

"You do your thing, and I'll do mine."

The fetters snap, for pursuing the flower is more important than caring for the partner.

"I won't go your way because you won't go mine."

They remain together, but their journey ceases. Each new moment that unfolds is filled with longing for that flower out of reach and is wasted by blaming the partner. Though the fetters are intact, the creative covenant withers.

"You do your thing, and I'll give up mine."

The "giver" dons a large martyr medal and drags after the partner—a burden every step of the way. Again, the fetters remain, but the creative covenant fades.

"Let's go side by side, first one way and then the other."

Together they decide which way to go first, and they support each other fully in both endeavors. Their creative covenant is renewed.

Again and again partners make decisions. Some partners snap their fetters; others stagnate where they are, looking longingly toward the top of the mountain. In some marriages, one partner becomes a martyr living in the shadow of the other. But there are also marriages that are strengthened because the partners actualize their care for one another—sharing pain and pleasure and joy and sorrow, struggling and growing together.

As the years go by, they climb on, renewing their covenant and passing others by. But there comes a time when the wife stumbles over an insurmountably difficult personal obstacle and desperately needs the help of her husband. In that moment, he has two choices. He can remove the fetters and hurry on, occasionally glancing back over his shoulder at her. Or, the arm of the stronger can be placed around the shoulders of the weaker—giving, caring, coaxing her toward continued growth. And then that moment is exchanged for another, which finds the stronger now the weaker, as the stumbling husband needs the help of his wife. And she also has two choices. She may leave him behind, or, not in duty but in love, put her arm around him—likewise giving, caring, coaxing him toward continued growth.

Weary from their long hard climb, yet knowing deep satisfaction, they make the last few steps to the top of the mountain—and gasp at what they see. For stretching ruggedly into the sky is another mountain!

And so, I dream of two partners climbing all the mountains they can, freely fettered together, caring for each other, responsibly helping each other grow, joyfully—and sometimes sorrowfully—experiencing the kind of interpersonal communion that only a covenant relationship can provide.

So it is in our life with God. We decide to climb all the

mountains we can—caring for the other climbers and for the climb itself in keen awareness that we are one with the Creator. And in this awareness, the strain of the effort is eased. Thomas Kelly, in *A Testament of Devotion,* says:

> Strain! Strain! Out of such attitudes are built those lives which get written up in the success-stories of the *American Magazine.* And religious people think they must work hard and please God and make a good record and bring in the kingdom![7]

The life with God is not the strained life, but neither is it one of escape from struggle. The life with God does not hide from reality behind a mask of piety, nor judge others from a pedestal of self-righteousness, nor distort the faith into a superstitious good luck charm. The life with God struggles to create dreams, stumbles over mountainside obstacles, trips through the darkness of sorrow, and skips in the light of joy—ever sensitive to and sustained by the strengthening Presence of God. Kelly tells us:

> For the experience of Presence is the experience of peace, and the experience of peace is the experience not of inaction but of power, and the experience of power is the experience of a pursuing Love that loves its way untiringly to victory. He who knows the Presence knows peace, and he who knows peace knows power and walks in complete faith that that objective Power and Love which has overtaken him will overcome the world.[8]

In the life with God, an interpersonal communion is experienced that only a covenant relationship can provide.

The masses are going to look at their relationships, their commitments, and their faith, and decide to plant radishes. But there will always be among them God's remnant who dare to plant date trees—those men and women of faith with the courage to covenant.

VI
The Courage
to be the Church

Again, Pilot takes charge: One of us must go today. And tomorrow, another . . . Pilot looks at the aeronautical map and tries to explain where they are and where to go: Follow the flow . . . He offers his map. Go . . . Down . . .

Son and Friend shake hands. If we're still here tomorrow . . . Their eyes meet and hold. . . . Tomorrow, I'll try to follow . . . Friend wears Father's coat for extra warmth.

Mother slowly raises her finger and points toward the food basket. Take . . . Her weakened voice is barely audible.

Friend reaches into the basket. A few crackers and a grape crush remain. He holds them in his hands—familiar words come to his mind:

This is my body broken for you. . . .
This is my blood spilled for you. . . .

The courage to be the church—that could mean a number of different things to different people. Our perspective depends upon our theological stance, personal experiences, and specific community of faith. Let's approach the courage to be the church from four dimensions of action—to confess, to celebrate, to be creative, and to covenant.

As the Body of Christ where do we begin in the confession of our shortcomings! May God forgive us. Our confession could become a multivolume work in itself, but for the moment, let us confess just one of our shortcomings: We lack the courage to live out those beliefs that reflect the continuing emergence of God.

We seem unaware that faith is dynamic rather than static, flowing rather than fixed. A few years ago, there was a man in my church school class who got terribly upset everytime someone said something about God that did not fit his limited interpretation. Each Sunday I found myself wondering if he became so upset—or threatened—because he lacked confidence in the God he so adamantly defended. As if a whisper could whiff his God away. Pirsig reminds us:

> No one is fanatically shouting that the sun is going to rise tomorrow. They *know* it's going to rise tomorrow. When people are fanatically dedicated to political or religious faiths or any other kinds of dogmas or goals, it's always because these dogmas or goals are in doubt.[1]

A rigid narrow perception of God that remains unquestioned is comforting. The cost, however, is that our faith also remains unbroadened—our concept of God becomes static rather than dynamic. God stands in awesome glory, majesty, and power, continually emerging, and when we are open to growth in this area, our image of God changes.

There was a time when God was viewed as a stern unsmiling father, and the godly life was the joyless life. Rupert Brooke caught this image in "Song of the Children in Heaven":

And when on whistles and toy drums
We make a loud amusing noise,
Some large official seraph comes
And scolds, and takes away our toys,
Bids us sit still and be good boys.

And when a baby laughs up here
Or rolls his crown about in play,
There is a pause. God looks severe;
The Angels frown, and sigh and pray,
And some-one takes the crown away.[2]

Though most communities of faith have moved beyond perceiving God as a stern unsmiling father and away from viewing the godly life as one that excludes joy, still among us are the frowners who cannot conceive of the whimsical, the gleeful, or even of laughter itself as dimensions given us by the Creator. Kelly says: "I'd rather be a jolly Saint Francis hymning his canticle to the sun than a dour old sobersides Quaker whose diet would appear to have been spiritual persimmons."[3] The beliefs of the frowners do not reflect the continuing emergence of God.

There was also a time when we focused so much on God that we tripped over our neighbor without even noticing. And then in the sixties, the pendulum jerked in the other direction. Alves tell us:

Christians discovered a new meaning for their faith. . . . No longer the opiate of the people, religion became suddenly an instrument of liberation. Perhaps the Church could be transformed into a revolutionary community! Perhaps the hour was at hand for her to become the midwife of a new future for mankind. And those who had exchanged their religious faith for a political ideology lived their ideologies with true religious fervor and found in their action groups the communal and messianic meaning they longed for.
Again hopes were followed by frustration.[4]

We focused on the neighbor—on social issues—forgetting the One in whose name we were to give the cups of cold water. Jesus modeled the importance of both the Creator and the created, and when, as the Body of Christ, our beliefs espouse one without the other, they do not reflect the continuing emergence of God.

Throughout history people have attempted not only to explain God, but also to explain God away: "Feuerbach explained God away in terms of the infinite desire of the human heart; Marx explained him away in terms of an ideological attempt to rise above the given reality; Nietzsche as a weakening of the will to live."[5] We are too ignorant, too blind, too insensitive, either to explain God or to explain God away. We can only speak in symbols, for God reaches beyond, behind, and above our limited language. When, as the Body of Christ, we think we've "found it"—that we have God all wrapped up neatly in a pretty little box, that we can fully and finally define God, or feel threatened when someone speaks of God in a new or different way from ours—when we think we can explain God or explain God away—then our belief is limited to a god that is a rigid and static imitation of the eternally emerging Creator.

Each of us is blessed with a glimpse, nothing more. Some people seem able to focus on their glimpse with more clarity and to speak more profoundly than the rest of us. Thomas Kelly and Paul Tillich are two of these people. We would expect to find little similarity between a Quaker mystic's glimpse of God and that of an existential theologian; however, there are startling parallels. When Kelly speaks of God, he speaks of Presence; Tillich speaks of being-itself. Both theologians are concerned with our anxiety. Kelly speaks simply of the strained life and the anecdote of peace;

Tillich goes through an ontology and typology of anxiety. Kelly has us look inside and outside—within ourselves and then outward toward our brothers and sisters. He says in his quietly powerful way:

> There is a way of life so hid with Christ in God that in the midst of the day's business one is inwardly lifting brief prayers, short ejaculations of praise, subdued whispers of adoration and of tender love to the Beyond that is within. . . .
>
> Now out from such a holy Center come the commissions of life. Our fellowship with God issues in world-concern. We cannot keep the love of God to ourselves. It spills over. It quickens us. It makes us see the world's needs anew.[6]

Tillich has us look above and beyond. He speaks of the God above the God of theism and the God beyond God. He speaks of faith: "Absolute faith [is] the state of being grasped by the God beyond God, . . . "[7] Tillich also speaks of the church:

> But a church which raises itself in its message and its devotion to the God above the God of theism without sacrificing its concrete symbols can mediate a courage which takes doubt and meaninglessness into itself. It is the Church under the Cross which alone can do this, the Church which preaches the Crucified who cried to God who remained his God after the God of confidence had left him in the darkness of doubt and meaninglessness. To be as a part in such a church is to receive a courage to be in which one cannot lose one's self and in which one receives one's world.[8]

It is this kind of community of faith whose beliefs reflect the continuing emergence of God.

And it is this kind of community of faith that will have the courage to be the church in the future. Perhaps someday my children's children will come to me and say, "Grandmother, your God is too small. God is not just the God above God. The God of the Church under the Cross is beyond the God beyond God!" And if so, I hope I will be able to make room in my soul to celebrate this, to recognize that the ancient symbols—which will still stand—point to an even larger God than I had ever dreamed.

After confession the next dimension of action is celebration. Incorporated in the courage to be the church is not only an awareness of our need for confession, but also an understanding of who we are as the Body of Christ. And with this understanding, comes celebration. As communities of faith, we celebrate Presence in the present.

To *celebrate*. To come together as a community of faith on Sunday morning. Or is it to come together as a congregation on Sunday, *mourning*. Too often it seems to be the latter. The dim lights, slow music, muted voices, preacher's eulogy. It is a rehearsal—not of life—but of death. And *this* some churches dare to call worship! As communities of faith, we respond to the miracle of God's love and the marvel of life by coming together in joyful, exhilarating *celebration*.

To celebrate Presence. Presence is a beautiful word, a peaceful word, a comforting word. It is paradise. As communities of faith, we know Presence in our solemn and serene sanctuaries, where the sun shines through brilliant stained-glass windows, reflecting their colors on a soft scarlet carpet. We know Presence in the steeple that stands high above the city and in the polished gold cross on the altar.

But wait. We see Jesus Christ carrying a rough hewn wooden cross. We hear nails piercing flesh. We smell vinegar. And, suddenly, we are expelled from paradise—for we are aware that Presence is everywhere. The stained-glass windows of our soothing sanctuaries are thrown open, and we are forced to look outside at the real world—to see the poverty, hear the moans, smell the pollution, feel the choking closeness. We are required to open ourselves to feel with painful sensitivity the injustice and hurts and inequities that surround us. For, as the Body of Christ, we cannot hide from need; we are to be present with Presence.

To celebrate Presence in the present. As congregations, we tend to march boldly into the nineteenth century. We protect ourselves from the confusing complexities of the present by entrenching ourselves in the past. At least some congregations do. Others are like insurance companies dealing in post death policies. They modify congregational behavior by threatening the punishment of hell and offering the reward of heaven. (This is the psychological stick-and-carrot theory institutionalized and disguised as "faith"!) The first group is focusing on the past, and the latter on the future. Neither is celebrating Presence in the *present.*

To me Holy Communion is symbolic of celebrating Presence in the present. As I go to the table of the Lord and kneel at the altar and hear the words of loving concern, I feel my children by my side and glance around the communion table at the others kneeling there. I see women with soft warm eyes framed by smile wrinkles. Their eyes hold that sparkle often seen in persons who spend their lives sowing good seeds. And I see men kneeling also—men with a gentleness that comes from strength. I see my brothers and sisters in the faith that I've come to care for deeply, sensitive persons for whom a caring response is a habit. Around that table we take a moment to celebrate Presence in the present. And then, with the commission, "Go in peace, and may the peace of God go with you," we rise, strengthened in that moment with renewed courage to be the church.

The church with the courage to lengthen that moment into a faith-stance continues in communion —corporately as the Body of Christ and individually as Christians. As the table of the Lord, the communion table is expanded to the table of the universe, excluding no one. Kneeling as stewards before the Creator of all, we remove the masks our fear projects upon others as well as the ones we hide behind ourselves, and we look around the table at the rich and the poor, the black and the white, the self-seeking and self-sacrificing, the young and the old, the busy and the bored, the loved and the lonely, and we hear and speak words of loving concern. As the Body of Christ incarnate, we celebrate Presence in the present.

To speak of being creative as a community of faith, is to risk being totally misunderstood, for there is much confusion in this area. To be creative as a community of faith does not mean playing "Can you top this?" every Sunday morning, nor copying another church's style of worship or programming, nor pretending there is no need for the traditional reminders that we are the chosen and the choosing people, set apart to live our lives under God. When a community of faith is creative, it reaches toward its corporate potential and becomes the unique expression of the Body of Christ that only it can be.

Time and time again, churches seem to entrap themselves in two snares that block creativity—repetition and reaction. Some churches fear the change that creativity brings. A clue to their fear is their ritualistic response to any new suggestion: "But we've done it *this* way for years." And they continue to do it that way for still more years—like animals biologically doomed to repeat their patterns of behavior generation after generation. But it doesn't have to be that way. The future of the church is open. The creative act can occur in *any* congregation with *any* minister. Remember Tillich's statement that a particular group would not be the same without each *individual self*. Each combination of people is unique. When a particular minister with his or her specific individual gifts reaches out to a particular congregation with its specific corporate gifts, and together they explore and express their special unique combination, we find—not repetition —but the creative act.

The second snare is reaction. Some churches seem to drain their energy and time—precious moments that can never again be relived—in a swirl of demonic tension. The pastor discounts the parish, and the parish discounts the pastor. We've all seen ministers and congregations who, instead of exploring and expressing the uniqueness of their combination, choose to become interlocked in reaction against each other. The result is not creative tension but demonic destruction.

Nikolai Berdyaev's understanding of revolution can be applied to the Body of Christ: "It is an illusion that revolution breaks with the old. It is only that the old makes its appearance with a new mask on. The old slavery changes its dress, the old inequality is transformed into new inequality."[9] Any act which is solely concerned with the negation of something, or someone is self-defeating. It kills rather than creates new life.

The community of faith that continually acknowledges itself to be made up of people living under God—the chosen and choosing ones reaching toward the One—that corporately strives towards its potential and creatively blossoms into a unique and authentic expression of the Body of Christ—is the community of faith that will have the courage to be the church.

All that has been said about the courage to be the church—confession, celebration, and creativity—is dependent upon a community being covenanted together. Too often the people within a church are anything but covenanted together, and one is reminded of the park depicted by Pirsig: "People entered the park and became polite and cozy and fakey to each other because the atmosphere of the park made them that way."[10] Or, to be more specific: "People entered the [church] and became polite and cozy and fakey to each other because the atmosphere of the [church] made them that way." In such a church, the Body of Christ has not covenanted together.

Later Pirsig speaks of the college classroom: "This was a place where he was *received*—as himself. Not as he could be or should be but as himself. A place all receptive. . . . "[11] Isn't this our desire in a community of faith—to be received, and therefore to receive? Such is the Body of Christ covenanted together.

To get hold of the meaning of covenant, let's think about the creative covenant in marriage—climbing up mountains, freely fettered together—and translate that dream to the community of faith. I dream that members of a community of faith are covenanting to climb life's mountains freely fettered together. The fetters are flexible, allowing individual freedom and creativity. They are retained by choice—and the covenant renewed. Or by choice removed—and the covenant broken. Freely fettered together as one body—as one unique expression of the Body of Christ—the community of faith continues its stumbling struggle, its journey of joy. Here again, there is a need for a common cadence, a flexible pace. It is a pace that does not allow moving backwards nor standing still, because that would be unfaithful to the One it calls Lord; but neither does it run off and leave behind the slowest or the weakest, or even the most obstinate member of the community of faith. It puts its communal arms around that member, too, caring and coaxing him or her toward continued growth.

Suddenly, part of the community is attracted in another direction and wants to turn off the trail and blaze a new one of its own; the rest of the church family wants to keep to the traditional path. The fetters will stretch and accommodate this distance until they become taut, and then the limits are reached. The small group must decide whether it will leave the new mission behind and rejoin the main body; stay with the mission and break the covenant to the main body, ceasing the climb; or, try to take up that mission and make it part of the concern of the entire community of faith.

And the main body must decide whether it will wait for the faction to return; leave it behind, cutting it off and breaking the covenant; or, support the new mission, carrying this new responsibility along with it as the members continue their climb, covenant intact.

The creative community of faith will have many small groups attracted in many different directions, and each time a decision must be made by the faction and by the main body, whether to break or to renew, the covenant.

The community of faith will overcome—or be defeated by—jealousy, impatience, mistrust, rigidity, narrow vision. For some—many?— communities of faith, the climb up the mountain will cease. And they will become a closed community of domesticated fat ducks flapping their wings without purpose, going no place. Other communities of faith will splinter, breaking their covenant, snapping the fetters that bind them together, becoming fragmented into intolerant ingrown social or political groups without a holistic faith, a common focal point, or a central goal in climbing God's mountains. But there are also those communities of faith whose journey together will continue, and it will be a colorful one, a creative one, enriched by broadened mission and mutual support and the pain and joy of growth. Covenanted together in the name of Jesus Christ, they will climb one mountain after another.

According to Alves, when we discover

> that we share similar hopes, that we participate in the same symphony of groans, are willing to risk our lives for the creation of a world we both love, we may clasp hands, embrace, and kiss each other. . . . And how beautiful it is when this discovery takes place! Words become unnecessary. Even silence communicates. Because in our silence our eyes and hearts are set on a common horizon. Love which takes place only in the immediacy of the present is a lie; it cannot endure.[12]

Our love as Christians steps back in time to our Book, our history, our creeds, our traditions. It steps forward in time to envision the kingdom of God.

There are many more dimensions to be considered when we ponder the courage to be the church. But for the purposes of this writing, let it suffice to say that we cannot be the church unless we are aware of the shortcomings of our individual communities of faith and confess them; that we cannot be the church unless we understand our communities of faith to be the Body of Christ and celebrate both the freedom and responsibility that this entails; that we cannot be the church unless we choose as communities of faith to be under God, utilizing our corporate power of creativity to build a more Christ-like world; and that we cannot be the church unless we covenant with God as individual communities of faith—which can only be symbolized by our mutual covenanting together as individual members.

VII

The Courage to Care

Once when I was ill with a stomach virus, our daughter Valerie came upstairs smiling and carrying a tray. "I made you some jello, Mom. It'll make you feel better." It was a small thing, and yet, very special to me. For years I'd been making jello for the children when they were ill, and now it had been made for me. We looked at each other a moment—a meaningful moment that will stay with me in memory, to be called forth when needed to warm a lonely day. It felt good to be cared for. As the cold softness slipped down my throat, I realized it was the best jello I'd ever eaten—but then, something given in love is always special.

Soon after, at a ministers' wives' retreat that I was leading, we did a word association exercise with the word "sorrow." One sensitive young woman responded "missed opportunities." Each morning we awake with the possibility of giving ourselves in love, and yet we speed unseeing through the day, and finally go to bed at night—having missed opportunities to make jello for someone. And that day's opportunities are forever gone.

Pirsig reflects on our loss:

> I watch the cars go by for a while on the highway. Something lonely about them. Not lonely—worse. Nothing. Like the attendant's expression when he filled the tank. Nothing. . . .
>
> Something about the car drivers too. They look just like the gasoline attendant, staring straight ahead in some private trance of their own. . . . They all look like they're in a funeral procession. . . .
>
> The cars seem to be moving at a steady maximum speed for in-town driving, as though they want to get somewhere, as though what's here right now is just something to get through. The drivers seem to be thinking about where they want to be rather than where they are. . . .
>
> The funeral procession! The one everybody's in, this hyped-up, . . . supermodern, ego style of life that thinks it owns this country.[1]

The funeral procession passes along the mountainside. Blank faces on lonely people. Confusing rocks with treasure, they load them into their backpacks. Their burdens grow heavier each step of the way, but the familiar emptiness is not filled. Ignoring others —ignored by them. Uncaring—uncared for.

Here a line from a poem by William Dickey is appropriate:

> Alone, I care for myself as for a body
> someone left here by accident.[2]

The funeral procession stumbles by. A procession of mass humanity isolated from one another, multiple islands of egocentricity, confusing self-interest with self-care. Each island is interested in the admiration of others rather than the actualization of self. Each is dwarfed by missed opportunities. Each marches along in a parade of the walking dead.

The New Yorker's "Talk of the Town" comments that our society has disintegrated

> from one that strengthens the bonds between people to one that is, at best, indifferent to them; . . . more and more, the old bonds are seen not as enriching but as confining.

The "self" words are stressed,

> "self-awareness," "self-fulfillment," "self-discovery," "self-determination," and "self-sufficiency"—terms that crowd anybody other than the "self" right out of one's imagination. . . . (When the relationship—no matter how good—gets in the way of self-fulfillment, it is clear which one has to go.)

One side of human awareness is

> the passionate loneliness at the center of each destiny, . . . But the other side—that we give form and meaning to those solitary destinies through our associations with others—has been allowed to fade away, leaving us exposed to a new kind of cold.[3]

Our "What-about-me?" hedonism with its frantic search for meaning through self-indulgence and freedom without responsibility has overlooked a traditional basic truth. A continual "What about me?" will send us again and again down the wrong fork in the path. "What about *you?*" is the question—but it is imperative that it arise from a healthy self-concept, and not from martyrdom. Life becomes meaningful as we become concerned about the other. The *giving* life is the *living* life.

Before we judge the hedonists outside the church too harshly, let's peek for a moment inside the church. We see people kneeling in prayer. Listen. One is praying to her Cosmic Candyman—"Dear God, gimmie." Another, who returns to the altar when his life needs repair is praying to his Mighty Mechanic—"Dear God, fix it." Another is exhibiting the gift of glossolalia. All of them have forgotten the *other*. Their self-interest is as evident as that of the secular hedonist. They too, have overlooked the traditional basic truth.

Viktor Frankl says it well: "The meaning which a being has to fulfill is something beyond himself, it is never just himself."[4] If we are unable to care for anyone or anything *separate from* ourselves, we are unable to care fully *for* ourselves. Materialism and power cannot fill the stagnant void felt in the funeral procession.

Andras Angyal tells us, "We are motivated to search not only for what we ask and need but also for that for which we are needed, what is wanted from us."[5] From a writer, artist, or scientist, it is a thing that is needed—a poem or novel, a painting, an invention. From poetess Phillis Wheatley, a few lines of "On Imagination" serve as an example:

> Though Winter frown, to Fancy's raptured eyes
> The fields may flourish, and gay scenes arise;
> The frozen deeps may burst their iron bands,
> And bid their waters murmur o'er the sands.[6]

Such is the transforming power of imagination caught through the words of our first black poetess.

But for most of us, it is not through some*thing* that we serve, but through some*one*. I'll try to say it in verse:

Though darkness doom, through Caring's gentle touch
A sunbeam dances, and two hands clutch;
Old icy fear may cease its masquerade,
And new found courage sing in serenade.

Such is the transforming power of the courage to care, taught through the life of the One we call Lord.

And Carl Rogers states that "the degree to which I can create relationships which facilitate the growth of others as separate persons is a measure of the growth I have achieved in myself."[7]

We are intertwined with others, separate limbs of the same tree, rooted in the love of Jesus Christ. In living a caring life one finds that it is a stance with many dimensions. The three that I would like to lift up are affirmation, accountability, and authenticity.

Affirmation

It is common for us as parents, in an affluent, harried, materialistic culture to give our children things instead of giving them our time. We provide good food, fashionable clothes, and comfortable shelter; we give them all sorts of lessons and buy them things, and more things. Presents are confused with presence, and children stumble about in possession-filled prisons of poverty —unabandoned but unaffirmed.

Affirmation is essential to caring. It fosters a feeling of worth. It requires of us an unpreoccupied, active listening to one another, an awareness of ourselves and others, and an understanding of our own feelings and those of others—a sensitive sharing of life with one another.

Affirmation involves personal risk. Alves focuses on our reluctance to take this risk.

> Who are you? I am a businessman, I am a professor, I am a housewife, I am a garbage collector. I am what I do. But [one's] private diary, written in blood and tears, with grief and joy—[one's] highest thoughts about himself, the book of his hopes—[is] locked from the world. [8]

We protect ourselves from being known. The mask of fear falls between us and others, blocking relationships of depth and meaning and intimacy. Rollo May suggests:

> It is easier in our society to be naked physically than to be naked psychologically or spiritually—easier to share our body than to share our fantasies, hopes, fears, and aspirations, which are felt to be more personal and the sharing of which is experienced as making us more vulnerable. For curious reasons we are shy about sharing the things that matter most. [9]

Affirmation is not a one-way street, but flows to and from each individual. It involves supporting and being supported, touching and being touched, loving and being loved. In being affirmed, a person experiences affection that is not possessive, understanding that is not simply verbal but empathic, and positive regard that is unconditional—that accepts others, not as we want them to be, but as they are.

One day when our youngest son Bryant came home from school, I gave him a big hug and said, "Bryant, do you know what a joy you are?"

He looked at me with a twinkle in his blue eyes and replied, "Just call me J. J."

"J. J.?" I asked.

He nodded. "I'm a joy and a genius!"

To accept him as he is is to acknowledge that he is definitely a joy—but most assuredly not a genius.

As we receive affection, understanding, and positive regard, we learn to express the same to others. We learn what it means to be in full presence with one another—to participate in an I-am/You-are relationship.

Affirmation calls for an appreciation of humanity as a whole—the similarities we share in common and the differences that give our planet colorful variegation. Affirmation includes the ability to be a part of the world. To be with others in the ugliness of life, hand in hand in the darkness of night, bumping roughly over deep ruts scarred with treadmarks of weariness and chugholes of despondency—aware of the death in living. And also to be with others in the beauty of life, side by side in the early morning light, skipping joyfully over colorful winding lanes sparkling with the fresh dew of a new beginning—aware of the life in living. And to affirm the existence of both beauty and ugliness, both joy and sorrow, both living and dying. The affirming person knows struggle, but also celebration in the midst of that struggle.

Accountability

It is common in our permissive hedonistic culture for us as parents to say yes if other parents have said yes, for it is easier to follow along than to set family standards. Children are given freedom beyond their ability to handle it, without parents' teaching and expecting responsibility. A lack of limits is confused with love, and the children stagnate in their permissive prisons.

In caring for others, affirmation is important, but so is accountability. Just as affirmation includes the ability to be a part of the world, so accountability includes the strength to be apart from it when values clash. To continue to call names when computers call numbers. To see "losing" as a means of growth when "winning" is the mode of the day. To grow roots when the norm is rootlessness. To recognize responsibility for the global family. To dare to actualize a "What-about-*you*?" philosophy in a "What-about-me?" world. To risk permanence in the midst of the temporary and to be close where there is structured distance. The accountable person stands like a sturdy spruce among the quaking aspens.

Accountability develops responsibility. It is not hierarchical, but reciprocal. We are accountable to and for members of our immediate, church, and world families. As accountable persons we reach out in responsible love, undergirded by the recognition of strength in one another and by the knowledge that we all have the ability to change. Accountability requires us to face limitations and obstacles, to bear the consequences of our behavior, and to realize our capacity for conflict as well as for resolving conflict. As we experience responsible love, we recognize the difference between legitimate individual needs and excessive self-interest. Each of us can act out the realization that "I am not the only one in my immediate,church, or world family; everyone else is fully a member also."

The life-space of the faithful Christian is consumed neither in perpetually singing "Fill My Cup, Lord," totally oblivious to anyone else—nor in frantically filling the cups of others, painfully sensitive to our thirst-crazed world. Whereas some of us refuse to come out of the prayer closet long enough to act out our prayers, others of us live under the illusion that the faithful life is the life that squeezes in one more thing—one more project, one more meeting, one more service. Not long ago, Bill gave the invocation at a banquet honoring the teachers of the year from communities across Oklahoma. Being named the top teacher in his or her community was a high honor for each teacher there—for many, no doubt, the highest honor of a lifetime. The state teacher of the year was also to be named, and the dinner was a significant event for each of the teachers. Not so, however, for the overburdened people at the head table. The distraught master of ceremonies confused the introductions (omitting the president-elect of the state teachers' organization); the harried man that called out the list of teachers as they received their awards did not synchronize each name with the presentation of the appropriate award; and the overcommitted speaker even forgot to bring his speech. Sometimes it becomes clear that we are busy-busying our lives away, as though driven by a need to collect do-gooder points. John Powell speaks to this.

> Being a loving person is far different from being a so-called "do-gooder." Do-gooders merely use other people as opportunities for practicing their acts of virtue, of which they keep careful count. People who love learn to move the focus of their attention and concern from themselves out to others. They care deeply about others. The difference between do-gooders and people who love is the difference between a life which is an on-stage performance and a life which is an act of love.[10]

Ouch, that stings.

Our motivation makes the difference. Some people walk on stage and dramatically exhibit their love for God. But there are also those who quietly reach toward others, living out their entire lives loving others—not paternalistically out of pity—but in response to the awesome, wondrous love of God expressed in Jesus Christ. This is caring for others in a new way because our perception has changed. Kelly says:

> We enfold them in our love, and we and they are enfolded together within the great Love of God as we know it in Christ. Once walk in the Now and men are changed, in our sight, . . . They aren't just masses of struggling beings, furthering or thwarting our ambitions, or, in far larger numbers, utterly alien to and insulated from us. We become identified with them and suffer when they suffer and rejoice when they rejoice.[11]

He speaks of the special people close to us, for "in the foreground arise special objects of love and concern and tender responsibility. The people we know best, see oftenest, have most to do with, these are *reloved* in a new and deeper way."[12]

Our world is too vast and our lifetime too short to carry all responsibilities. Kelly says that God "never guides us into an intolerable scramble of panting feverishness."[13] He reminds us that

> the Loving Presence does not burden us equally with all things, but considerately puts upon each of us just a few central tasks, as emphatic responsibilities. For each of us these special undertakings are our share in the joyous burdens of love. . . .
> I wish I might emphasize how a life becomes simplified when dominated by faithfulness to a few concerns. Too many of us have too many irons in the fire. We get distracted by the intellectual claim to our

interest in a thousand and one good things, and before we know it we are pulled and hauled breathlessly along by an over-burdened program of good committees and good undertakings. I am persuaded that this fevered life of church workers is not wholesome. . . . The concern-oriented life is ordered and organized from within. And we learn to say *No* as well as *Yes* by attending to the guidance of inner responsibility.

We learn to be accountable.

Authenticity

Our success-oriented, Dale-Carnegie culture fosters an excessive fear of failure. As parents and grandparents, we sometimes get caught up in this and focus on image rather than on intimacy, reinforcing appearance rather than authenticity, learned superficiality rather than natural spontaneity. Like forcing a budding Picasso to restrict his free flourishes to a paint-by-number copy of another's work, children's colorful and creative expressions of uniqueness are discounted, inhibited, and hidden. They shrivel in a prison of pretense.

Authenticity is an indispensable dimension of caring, for it provides us with an opportunity to be ourselves in the presence of others, with our smiles and strengths as well as our warts and weaknesses. Authenticity requires courage, for the masks of fear have long separated us, confining us to the safety of games and the propriety of roles. Pirsig gives us a sketch: "Hundreds of itsy-bitsy rules for itsy-bitsy people. . . . It was all table manners, not derived from any sense of kindness or decency or humanity."[14]

We spend a great deal of energy substituting

pretense for personhood. As parents, however, we will probably not be able to get by with this, for others will see in our children who we really are. We may be careful to mouth one set of standards, but sometimes we model quite another. Our children are not a reflection of our pronouncements and pretensions—they are the declaration of our actions and attitudes. As a friend once said to me, "Children are the report cards of their parents." When we free ourselves from the bondage of itsy-bitsy rules and from the molds designed for us by others, then we can enjoy spontaneity and express our God-given uniqueness.

Authenticity in caring for others requires us to be open and honest, self-disclosing and nondeceptive, straightforward and nonmanipulative. It includes a sense of identity and the ability and courage to express that identity. Emerson says: "Insist on yourself; never imitate. Your own gift you can present every moment with the cumulative force of a whole life's cultivation; of the adopted talent of another you have only an extemporaneous half possession." Authenticity calls us to struggle with the age-old questions that Abraham Maslow referred to.

What is the good life? The good man? The good woman?

What is best for our children? How can we live zestful, enjoyable, meaningful lives? What is our relation to nature, to death, to pain, to illness?

What is our responsibility to our brothers and sisters? Who are our brothers and sisters?

What is the good society and our relation and obligation to it? What is justice? Truth? Virtue?

What shall we be loyal to? What must we be ready to die for?

The authentic person—like a rare diamond found in

the midst of rhinestones—lives out the answers he or she has chosen to these questions.

It was noted earlier that we are intertwined in the love of Jesus Christ. We care deeply for some persons, less so for others. But whatever the degree of our caring, all our relationships hold in common the inevitability of termination. Whether through the passage of time, mobility, or death, at some point the relationship will cease to be what it is now. For example, some day Valerie will grow up and go away. And yet, I will always think of her when I see strawberry jello. We have only the moment, but it is a moment filled with opportunity, a moment that builds on the foundation of the past and forms memories to hold for the future.

As persons intertwined in the love of Jesus Christ, our care is not divisive, but inclusive. One of the events in American history that still chills my blood is the 1914 attack on the striking miners and their families in Ludlow, Colorado. Evicted from company housing, the miners were living in a tent colony at the edge of town. The state militia, including strikebreakers from the east in Colorado uniforms, advanced on the tents with torches and machine guns that were loaded with exploding bullets. The oldest victim was John Bartolotte, forty-five; the youngest was Elvira Valdez, a babe of three months. The miner who led the strike was shot fifty-one times and his body left exposed.

I decided to include this event in a historical novel that I'm writing. I took myself back in time to the Ludlow massacre, mentally and emotionally. As I wrote, I felt I was there—seeing the advancing uniforms, smelling the scorching heat of the burning tents, hearing the screams of the children, feeling the pain of the helpless miners. I *despised* the cruel coal barons.

After completing that scene, I began to prepare for a retreat I was to lead. Still feeling a passionate empathy for the miners' children and a seething hatred for the greedy coal barons, I came upon the following passage by Kelly:

> There is a tendering of the soul, toward *everything* in creation, from the sparrow's fall to the slave under the lash. The hard-lined face of a money-bitten financier is as deeply touching to the *tendered* soul as are the burned-out eyes of miners' children, remote and unseen victims of his so-called success.[15]

This is the kind of love—inclusive and all-encompassing—that is exemplified in the life of Jesus Christ.

How different that life-style is from the funeral procession of egocentric human islands! Miracle of miracles—we have been shown a better way. Instead of stagnating in the funeral procession, we can decide to live our lives as Christian pilgrims, coming together as a community of faith with the courage to be the church, and going out to climb God's mountains, aware of the destination but aware also of the real goal—putting in good moments during the journey. Being willing to give the time to make jello and the energy to carry another's pack. Knowing that real pleasure is the giving of oneself, that real treasure is the relationship with the other, and that real power is the power of love.

It was young Friend who came out of the cache, who ventured forth to find the way. It was Friend who was willing to struggle through the rugged unknown, through the lonely, expansive, Zhivago-like winter whiteness of

*the wilderness—going out on behalf of the dead,
the paralyzed, the wounded. It was Friend who
had the courage to care.*

It will be God's remnant who comes out of the
cache-time, who ventures forth to find the way. It
will be God's remnant who is willing to struggle
through the lonely unknown—going out on behalf of
the living dead, the psychologically paralyzed, the
waiting wounded. It will be God's remnant who has
the courage to care.

Notes

I. COURAGE IN A CACHE-TIME

1. Rollo May, *The Courage to Create* (New York: W. W. Norton & Co., 1975), p. 13.

II. THE COURAGE TO CONFESS

1. Paul Tillich, *The Courage to Be* (New Haven: Yale University Press, 1952), pp. 89–90.
2. Robert 'M. Pirsig, *Zen and the Art of Motorcycle Maintenance* (New York: William Morrow & Co., 1974), p. 282.
3. *The Confessions of Saint Augustine,* trans. Albert C. Outler (Philadelphia: The Westminster Press, 1955), p. 59.
4. Quoted in *Time* (March 14, 1977), 70.
5. Pirsig, *Zen,* p. 215.
6. Antoine de Saint Exupéry, *The Little Prince* (New York: Harbrace Paperbound Library, 1971, [1943]), pp. 16–17.
7. Pirsig, *Zen,* p. 5.
8. Willard Gaylin, "Caring Makes the Difference," *Psychology Today,* (August, 1976), 38, 39.

III. THE COURAGE TO CELEBRATE

1. Pirsig, *Zen,* p. 7.
2. *Ibid.,* pp. 198–99.
3. Tillich, *Courage,* p. 87.
4. *Ibid.,* p. 88.

5. Pirsig, *Zen,* p. 388.
6. Ross Stagner, "The Psychology of Human Conflict," *The Nature of Human Conflict,* ed. E. McNeil (Mich. Univ. Center for research on conflict resolution. Englewood Cliffs, N.J.: Prentice-Hall, 1965), p. 48.
7. *Ibid.,* p. 50.
8. Hermann and Hermann (1962), cited in McNeil, *Human Conflict,* p. 157.
9. Malachi Martin *Three Popes and the Cardinal* (New York: Farrar, Straus & Giroux, 1972), p. 179.
10. Pirsig, *Zen,* p. 214.

IV. THE COURAGE TO CREATE

1. Martin E. Marty, "Getting Up for Ministry in a Settle-Down Time," *The Christian Ministry* (November, 1977), 6–10.
2. Rubem Alves, *Tomorrow's Child:* Imagination, Creativity, and the Rebirth of Culture (New York: Harper & Row, 1972), pp. 143–44.
3. *Ibid.,* p. 150.
4. *Ibid.,* p. 188.
5. Dory Previn, "I Can't Go On," *Search the Silence:* Poems of Self-Discovery, ed. Betsy Ryan (New York: Scholastic Magazines 1974), p. 65.
6. Alves, *Tomorrow's Child,* pp. 169–70.

V. THE COURAGE TO COVENANT

1. Margery Williams, *The Velveteen Rabbit* (Garden City, N.Y.: Doubleday & Co., 1958), p. 17.
2. Alves, *Tomorrow's Child,* p. 33.
3. Cited in *Time* (March 14, 1977), 70.
4. *Ibid.*
5. *Ibid.*
6. Aldous Huxley, *Brave New World* (New York: Harper & Brothers, 1946), p. 58.
7. Thomas R. Kelly, *A Testament of Devotion* (New York: Harper & Brothers, 1941), p. 102.
8. *Ibid.,* pp. 102-3.

VI. THE COURAGE TO BE THE CHURCH

1. Pirsig, *Zen,* p. 146.
2. Rupert Brooke, "Song of theChildren in Heaven," cited

in Arthur C. McGill, *The Celebration of Flesh:* Poetry in
Christian Life (New York: Association Press, 1964), p.
183.
3. Kelly, *Testament,* p. 92.
4. Alves, *Tomorrow's Child,* p. 184.
5. Tillich, *Courage,* p. 142.
6. Kelly, *Testament,* p. 122.
7. Tillich, *Courage,* p. 188.
8. *Ibid.*
9. Nikolai Berdyaev, *Slavery and Freedom* (New York:
Charles Scribner's Sons, 1944), p. 196.
10. Pirsig, *Zen,* p. 136.
11. *Ibid.,* p. 172.
12. Alves, *Tomorrow's Child,* p. 171.

VII. THE COURAGE TO CARE

1. Pirsig, *Zen,* pp. 319–20.
2. William Dickey, "Alone I Care for Myself," *Search the
Silence,* p. 50.
3. "The Talk of the Town," *The New Yorker* (August 30,
1976), 21–22.
4. Cited in Milton Mayeroff, *On Caring,* ed. Ruth Anshen
(New York: Harper & Row, 1972, [1971]), p. xiv.
5. *Ibid.*
6. Phillis Wheatley, "On Imagination." Excerpt cited in
Rufus Wilmont Griswold, *The Female Poets of America,*
III (Philadelphia: Carey and Hart, 1849), p. 32.
7. Cited in Mayeroff, *On Caring,* p. xiii.
8. Alves, *Tomorrow's Child,* p. 101.
9. May, *Courage to Create,* p. 18.
10. John Powell, *Fully Human, Fully Alive* (Niles, Ill.:
Argus Communications, 1976), p. 26.
11. Kelly, *Testament,* p. 99.
12. *Ibid.,* p. 100.
13. *Ibid.,* pp. 124, 109–10.
14. Pirsig, *Zen,* p. 177.
15. Kelly, *Testament,* p. 106.